Especially for
Pam

From
from Mary W

Date
Dec 2010

© 2010 by Barbour Publishing, Inc.

Written and compiled by Janice Hanna.

ISBN 978-1-60260-819-1

Published by Barbour Publishing, Inc., P.O. Box 719, Uhrichsville, Ohio 44683, www.barbourbooks.com

Our mission is to publish and distribute inspirational products offering exceptional value and biblical encouragement to the masses.

Member of the
Evangelical Christian
Publishers Association

Printed in China.

Blessings for Girlfriends

BARBOUR
PUBLISHING

Extremely Special

If I had one gift that I could give you, my friend,
it would be the ability to see yourself as others see
you, because only then would you know how extremely
special you are.

B. A. BILLINGSLY

A Blessing for My Friend

May you, my friend, know the love of the Father,
the love of family, and the love of true friends.
May these blessings inspire you to become all you
were meant to be so that you can effectively reach
your world for Christ.

Ages and Stages

Girlfriends are great at every age and every stage.
Whether you're in senior high or you're a senior
citizen, there's something rather remarkable about
finding a "kindred spirit," a true friend with whom
to share this season of your life.

Bubbling Over

Dear Lord, please bless my girlfriend with that "bubbling over" kind of joy today. May she know the happiness that walking in relationship with You can bring. Father, I'm so grateful for the joy she brings to me as a sister in Christ. May I never take that joy for granted.

Rekindling the Inner Spirit

In everyone's life, at some time, our inner fire goes out. It is then burst into flame by an encounter with another human being. We should all be thankful for those people who rekindle the inner spirit.

ALBERT SCHWEITZER

You Raise Me Up

When you meet someone who makes you feel
invincible, you've met a true friend. A real friend isn't
afraid to watch you succeed. She gives you wings to
fly and encourages you to be the very best you can be.
Praise God for friends who raise us up!

The Sweetness of Your Counsel

The heartfelt counsel of a friend is as sweet as perfume and incense.

PROVERBS 27:9 NLT

What a Gift!

Father, sometimes I forget what a gift my girlfriends are. You have sent each one into my life like a present wrapped with sparkly paper and satiny bows. May I always see them as the heavenly gifts they are!

The Sort of Friend

I'd like to be the sort of friend that you have been to me;
I'd like to be the help that you've been always glad to be;
I'd like to mean as much to you each minute of the day
As you have meant, old friend of mine, to me along
the way.

EDGAR A. GUEST

Swimming in the Deep End

Sometimes life can be a little scary, especially when we go through unexpected challenges. It's a bit like swimming in the deep end. Thank goodness for our girlfriends! They're just the life preservers we need to stay afloat when the waters get deep!

A Blessed Thing

A blessed thing it is for any man or woman to
have a friend, one human soul whom we can trust
utterly, who knows the best and worst of us,
and who loves us in spite of all our faults.

CHARLES KINGSLEY

Perspective

A good friend will help you put things in perspective. She won't let you make too much or too little out of life's troubles and will always remind you that "this, too, shall pass." Praise the Lord for perspective!

A Circle of Friends

Dear Lord, sometimes I feel like I can't navigate beyond the drama and trauma of my life. I'm so grateful for the friends You've placed in my circle. They keep me focused and lift my spirits when I'm down. Thank You so much for these precious women!

A Handful of Friends

I cannot even imagine where I would be today were it
not for that handful of friends who have given me a
heart full of joy. Let's face it, friends make life a lot
more fun.

CHARLES R. SWINDOLL

You Make Me Laugh

There's something irresistible about a friend who makes you laugh. She has that magical gift: the ability to put a smile on your face when nothing— or no one—else can. Spend some time laughing with your girlfriends today.

A Prism's Reflection

Friendship is like a prism through which the many variations of beauty are revealed in our lives.

ANONYMOUS

Daughter of God

Father, it's often hard to see myself the way You see me.
My girlfriends offer a constant reminder that I have
value. Because of their encouragement, I am starting
to see myself as a princess—the daughter of the Most
High God! Thank You for using girlfriends to remind
me, Lord.

Two Are Better Than One

Two are better than one, because they have a good return for their work: If one falls down, his friend can help him up. But pity the man who falls and has no one to help him up!

ECCLESIASTES 4:9–10 NIV

You've Got a Friend

There is a Friend who is greater than all of our girlfriends put together. The Creator of heaven and earth is the best Friend you could ever have. If you haven't already done so, why not take Him up on His offer of friendship today?

The Palm of My Hand

If I could reach up and hold a star for every time you made me smile, the entire evening sky would be in the palm of my hand.

UNKNOWN

No Fear!

Lord, sometimes I worry about the future. I'll admit it. But having my girlfriends around helps. They remind me that I'm not alone. With their help, I am learning to trust You with the unknown. Daily, they remind me that this road I'm on is an adventure!

Don't Worry, My Friend

Are you upset, little friend? Have you been lying
awake worrying? Well, don't worry. . .I'm here.
The floodwaters will recede, the famine will end,
the sun will shine tomorrow, and I will always be here
to take care of you.

CHARLIE BROWN (TO SNOOPY)

The Difficult Places

We often say, "Lord, I'll go where You want me to go and do what You want me to do," then find ourselves challenged by where life takes us. Thank goodness for you, my friend. With your hand in mine, going to the "tough" places is much easier.

24/7 Friends

Toss the clocks, girls! A true friend is one you can call on day or night. I'm so grateful for my 24/7 girlfriends. They make themselves available whenever I need a shoulder to cry on or someone to celebrate with. Praise the Lord for close friends who are always there.

Around the Clock

The Bible encourages us to pray without ceasing.
We are called to be in constant communication with
the Lord. Doesn't it thrill your heart to know that your
friends are adding their prayers to yours? Together,
you are invincible.

My Wish for You

This is my wish for you: comfort on difficult days,
smiles when sadness intrudes, rainbows to follow the
clouds, laughter to kiss your lips, sunsets to warm your
heart, hugs when spirits sag, beauty for your eyes to see,
friendships to brighten your being, faith so that you
can believe, confidence for when you doubt, courage
to know yourself, patience to accept the truth, love to
complete your life.

ANONYMOUS

A Friend after God's Own Heart

Lord, my prayer today is that I will be the kind of friend You long for me to be. Help me to see people through Your eyes. Make me kindhearted and caring. May my hands be Your hands and my feet Your feet. Give me Your words to speak, Father.

Top Secret

Ever have a secret you're just bursting to tell?
With whom can you share it? Is there one you trust
with the "big" stuff? Isn't it wonderful to have such a
close relationship with a girlfriend that you can share
top-secret information in safety?

A Completed Work

Being confident of this, that he who began a good work in you will carry it on to completion until the day of Christ Jesus.

PHILIPPIANS 1:6 NIV

Material-Free Girls

Sometimes when girlfriends get together, a lot of time is spent talking about material things—clothes, shoes, houses, cars, and so forth. Sometimes we even compare, which can be dangerous. Material possessions are fine, but they don't drive us. Let's make today a material-free day!

Chatterboxes

We are friends and I do like to pass the day with
you in serious and inconsequential chatter.
I wouldn't mind washing up beside you, dusting
beside you, reading the back half of the paper
while you read the front. We are friends and I
would miss you, do miss you and think
of you very often.

JEANETTE WINTERSON

Where Would I Be?

Lord, sometimes I wonder where I would be without my girlfriends. They serve as a buffer from life's many storms and keep me sane on days when everything is spinning out of control. How can I ever thank You for the blessing they have been to me?

Woven Webs

You have been my friend. That in itself is a
tremendous thing. I wove my webs for you because I
liked you. After all, what's a life, anyway? We're born,
we live a little while, we die. A spider's life can't help
being something of a mess, with all this trapping and
eating flies. By helping you, perhaps I was trying to
lift up my life a trifle. Heaven knows anyone's life can
stand a little of that.

FROM *CHARLOTTE'S WEB* BY E. B. WHITE

That's the Truth

Lord, thank You for sending my girlfriends to tell me things I didn't want to tell myself. Sometimes the truth hurts, but Your Word promises that the truth will set me free. Thanks for using my friends to help in that process.

Breath of Kindness

A friend is one to whom one may pour out all the
contents of one's heart, chaff and grain together,
knowing that the gentlest of hands will take and
sift it, keep what is worth keeping and with a
breath of kindness blow the rest away.

ARABIAN PROVERB

His Eye Is on the Sparrow

The Lord knows when a sparrow falls. . .and He cares. Our friends aren't as knowing, but there are those rare few who always seem to know when, like that little sparrow, we've taken a tumble. Their "eye" is on us, and their heart of caring is huge.

Inexpressible Comfort

Oh, the comfort—the inexpressible comfort of feeling safe with a person—having neither to weigh thoughts nor measure words, but pouring them all right out, just as they are, chaff and grain together; certain that a faithful hand will take and sift them, keep what is worth keeping, and then with the breath of kindness blow the rest away.

DINAH MARIA MULOCK CRAIK

Courage to Stand

Lord, thank You so much for the brave friends who've walked into my life at the very moment others have walked out. For many it took courage to stand with me in the darkness, but they never wavered. How can I ever thank You enough for these dear sisters?

Sharpened

As iron sharpens iron, so a man sharpens the
countenance of his friend.

PROVERBS 27:17 NKJV

Glass Half Full

Don't you love hanging out with optimists? They always see the glass as half full. They don't drag you down; on the contrary, they seem exceptionally gifted at lifting your head. Praise the Lord for optimists!

The Golden Rule

Lord, we know that You teach us to do unto others
as we would have them do unto us. Thank You for
sending friends who make that easy! My girlfriends
are so good to me, Father. It's a pleasure to reciprocate
their kindness!

Secure

Lord, thank You for friends who sharpen me but don't stab me in the back! They know just how much to share and when to share it. I'm grateful for both their input and the sense of security I have around them.

Drop by Drop

We cannot tell the precise moment when
friendship is formed. As in filling a vessel drop
by drop there is at last a drop which makes it run
over, so in a series of kindnesses there is at last
one which makes the heart run over.

JAMES BOSWELL

Transparent

Being transparent is hard, isn't it? Sometimes we don't want people to see our flaws. Isn't it great to have girlfriends we can be transparent around? Perhaps we're so encouraged to show "the real us" because we've seen their wrinkles, too!

To Catch You
When You Fall. . .

If all my friends were to jump off a bridge, I wouldn't
jump with them—I would be at the bottom to catch
them.

ANONYMOUS

United We Stand

Lord, what a blessing it is to have like-minded
girlfriends who walk in relationship with You!
They spur me on to do great things for Your kingdom.
Together, we feel invincible! Thank You for that
precious sisterhood.

A Whole New World

Each friend represents a world in us, a world
possibly not born until they arrive, and it is only
by this meeting that a new world is born.

ANAÏS NIN

Just as I Am

Isn't it great to have girlfriends who love you just the way you are? They're crazy about you. . .even when you make mistakes, when you wake up on the wrong side of the bed, or when you do or say the wrong things.

Selfless Love

Your love must be real. Hate what is evil, and hold
on to what is good. Love each other like brothers and
sisters. Give each other more honor than you want for
yourselves.

ROMANS 12:9–10 NCV

Lighting the Way

Father, I'm so glad You direct my path. And I'm grateful You use my friends to help light the way. They serve as personal tour guides: I can depend on their advice, guidance, and encouragement. What a blessing!

A Million Little Things

Friendship isn't a big thing—
it's a million little things.

UNKNOWN

Climb Every Mountain

Life is filled with mountains and valleys. Sometimes
it feels the mountains are too high to climb and the
valleys too low to maneuver. And then a girlfriend
begins to walk alongside me. She lifts my load and
reminds me that I can do anything through Christ who
strengthens me.

A Promise to My Friend

The word *friend* is more than just a label. It's a promise that I will stick with you, no matter what. Happy times, sad times, sickness, seasons of joy—I'll be there by your side.

Angels in Disguise

Lord, I often wonder if my girlfriends are truly angels in disguise. They always "happen" to show up at just the right time and lift me up when I'm weary. Thank You for sending the right person at the right time.

God's Most Perfect Gift

There's a miracle of friendship
that dwells within the heart,
And you don't know how it happens
or where it gets its start;
But the happiness it brings you
always gives a special lift,
And you realize that friendship
is God's most perfect gift.

ANONYMOUS

Accountability Partners

Don't you love friends who are willing to be
accountability partners? They don't mind being called
on—day or night—for advice and counsel. Best of all,
you know you're safe with these special friends. Thanks
for letting me make myself accountable to you.

A Long and Winding Road

The journey of life is truly a long and winding road. At times we don't know where it will take us. We do know, however, that traveling hand in hand with a friend steadies our feet for the journey and calms our nerves.

Be Strong and Courageous

Lord, I know that through You, I can be strong and courageous. I also know that having courageous friends helps! I'm so grateful for my friends. They lift me up when I'm weary and keep me going, even when I feel like I can't take another step.

Footprints on the Heart

Some people come into our lives, leave footprints
on our hearts, and we are never the same.

ANONYMOUS

Keep Those Prayers Coming!

For this reason, since the day we heard about you, we have not stopped praying for you and asking God to fill you with the knowledge of his will through all spiritual wisdom and understanding.

COLOSSIANS 1:9 NIV

Personalities

What does your circle of girlfriends look like? Does
it feature an eclectic mix of personalities—outgoing,
shy, loud, quiet, dependent, independent? How clever
of the Lord to merge such different personalities into
one circle so that we can learn from one another!

Comfort Zone

Girlfriends force us out of our comfort zone, often asking us to do the very things we're sure we can't. They cheer us on from the sidelines, convincing us that we had nothing to worry about in the first place!

Words Unspoken

Lord, sometimes I don't feel like talking to
anyone. I just want to be quiet. Thank You for
hearing me, even in the silence. And thank You for
my close friends, who seem to hear the words
I speak. . .and the ones I don't.

Wanted: True Friend

A true friend is the greatest of all blessings, and that
which we take the least care to acquire.

FRANÇOIS DE LA ROCHEFOUCAULD

In Sickness and in Health

Girlfriends have sticking power. They don't run for the hills when the going gets tough. In fact, they draw closer than ever—praying, loving, and caring. Aren't you grateful for the friends who have stuck with you in good times and in bad?

Pardon My House. . .

A best friend is someone you don't have to apologize
to for the way your house looks when she comes over.

RHONDA G. BEST

Through the Veneer

Lord, there are those special girlfriends who can
see through my veneer. They see through the smile
on my face to the pain in my eyes. Their gaze
pierces to my very soul. Thank You for friends
who don't pretend everything is okay when
it's really not.

May I Come In?

A friend is the one who comes in when the whole world has gone out.

GRACE PULPIT

Just Listen

The most basic and powerful way to connect to
another person is to listen. Just listen. Perhaps the
most important thing we ever give each other is our
attention. . . . A loving silence often has far more
power to heal and to connect than the most
well-intentioned words.

RACHEL NAOMI REMEN

Remember My Name

If you want to win friends, make it a point to remember them. If you remember my name, you pay me a subtle compliment; you indicate that I have made an impression on you. Remember my name and you add to my feeling of importance.

DALE CARNEGIE

Medicine to the Soul

Lord, thank You for the scripture that says a merry
heart is like medicine to my soul. I'm tickled by
that idea, especially when I think about the friends
You've placed in my path. They keep me merry,
even when life is challenging.

A Friend Who Cares

The friend who can be silent with us in a moment of despair or confusion, who can stay with us in an hour of grief and bereavement, who can tolerate not knowing, not curing, not healing and face with us the reality of our powerlessness, that is a friend who cares.

HENRI NOUWEN

Apology Accepted

Sometimes we find ourselves in a position where an apology is necessary. How glorious to get that "I'm sorry!" off your chest. And how wonderful to hear someone say, "I forgive you." Have you been putting off an apology? Perhaps today is the day!

Old Shoes

You know how comfortable an old pair of shoes can be? They're worn in and fitted to your feet. That's what it's like when you spend time with a true girlfriend: You feel completely comfortable with each other.

Comfortable Friendship

Father, thanks so much for giving me girlfriends I
can relax with and just be myself around.
This kind of comfortable friendship is Your gift
to me, Lord. May I never take it for granted.

Masterpiece of Nature

A friend may well be reckoned the masterpiece of
nature.

RALPH WALDO EMERSON

Living for Today

I love girlfriends who help me live for today. They're not hung up on the mistakes of yesterday and they're not worried about the what-ifs of tomorrow. They help me keep things in perspective. Praise the Lord for "today" girlfriends!

C'mon to My House

Girlfriends are always welcome. . .even if the house is messy, the baby needs changing, or the yard needs mowing. A true friend doesn't see all of that stuff anyway (and if she does, she just rolls up her sleeves and offers to help).

Arm Lifters

Father, my friends have been a tremendous
blessing in my life. They've lifted my arms when
I've been weary, and they've helped me do things I
couldn't do for myself. How can I ever thank You
for these arm lifters?

Blessed Are They. . .

"Blessed are the merciful, for they will be shown mercy.
Blessed are the pure in heart, for they will see God.
Blessed are the peacemakers, for they will be called
sons of God."

MATTHEW 5:7–9 NIV

All You Need Is Love

A true girlfriend offers the very best kind of love.
She sees beyond all imperfections. She is patient and
kind. Best of all, a true friend goes on giving, even
when she's "given out." Now, that's the definition of
friendship!

Lean on Me

Ever felt like you needed someone to lean on? Let me be your friend. Lean on me. God has placed me in your life—not just for this season, but for this reason. You won't take advantage of me if you lean on me. That's what friends do, after all. So c'mon! Lean!

Never-Ending Friendship

A circle is round; it has no end.
That's how long I want to be your friend!

ANONYMOUS

Pinned with a Star

When twilight drops her curtain down
And pins it with a star,
Remember that you have a friend
Though she may wander far.

FROM *ANNE OF GREEN GABLES* BY
LUCY MAUD MONTGOMERY

New Every Morning

Aren't you glad God's mercies are new every morning?
We can toss the stuff from yesterday (or a thousand
yesterdays) and look at today as being fresh and new.
And godly friends are great at keeping the past in the
past, where it belongs.

To Know Her Is to Love Her

Worried about your physical or emotional flaws?
Well, don't be. When you're around your girlfriends,
they don't care about silly things like cellulite,
wrinkles, or a few extra pounds. To know a girlfriend. . .
is to love her (in spite of any and all self-perceived flaws).

Forgiveness

Father, You are such a forgiving God. You see my
sins, my failures, and yet You forgive me through
the blood of Your Son. Thank You for that
forgiveness. . .and thank You for friends who offer
forgiveness when I mess up, as well.

Cement

Friendship is the only cement that will ever hold the world together .

WOODROW WILSON

Pepper-in-the-Teeth Friendship

We depend on our closest friends to be brutally honest with us about those "awkward" things: "Your bra straps are showing." "You've got your shirt on inside out." "You've got pepper in your teeth." I'm so glad you're *that* kind of friend to me!

Don't Worry

"Therefore I tell you, do not worry about your life, what you will eat or drink; or about your body, what you will wear. Is not life more important than food, and the body more important than clothes?"

MATTHEW 6:25 NIV

Thick-Skinned Friendship

Lord, You've helped me get over my sensitivities so that I don't get my feelings hurt so easily whenever misunderstandings come up with my friends. I'm grateful for that, Father! May I always be the sort of friend who is known for being slow to get upset and quick to forgive.

The Right Questions

A true friend will ask you all the right questions and
not get angry if you don't give her all the right answers.

ARLENE LEWIS MULLER

Like-Minded

Whenever you spend time with a like-minded friend, it's like getting the two-for-one special. Your thoughts are linked. Your ideas meld. You enjoy the same movies and eat at the same restaurants. How fun to be so "in tune" with a good friend!

Just in Time

Aren't you grateful for those friends who show up "just in time" and walk you through life's struggles?
They seem to have an uncanny sense of timing and just "know" when you need them. Today, thank the Lord for those "just in time" friends.

Perfect Timing

Lord, Your timing is perfect. And I'm thankful for
friends who have great timing, too. I know their
presence in my life is not an accident. You send
them to me just when I need them most.
Thank You, Father!

Forever Friends

Even though we've changed and we're all finding our own place in the world, we know that when the tears fall or the smile spreads across our face, we'll come to each other, because no matter where this crazy world takes us, nothing will ever change so much to the point where we're not all still friends.

ANONYMOUS

Sticky Friends

Some friends only stick around when things are going well. Isn't it wonderful to find a friend who will stick with you whether things are going great or falling apart? These "sticky" friends are one of life's greatest blessings.

An Encouraged Heart

May our Lord Jesus Christ himself and God our
Father, who loved us and by his grace gave us eternal
encouragement and good hope, encourage your hearts
and strengthen you in every good deed and word.

2 THESSALONIANS 2:16–17 NIV

Encouragement

Lord, where would I be without encouragement?
Thank You for stepping in and encouraging me
when I'm down, and thank You for my friends,
who are the best encouragers I know! May I be
that sort of friend to others.

A Need for Friendship

And my God will meet all your needs according to his
glorious riches in Christ Jesus.

PHILIPPIANS 4:19 NIV

Singin' in the Rain

Girlfriends help us laugh, even when we don't have
a reason to. They have an uncanny ability to make
everything okay. . .even when it's really not. Today,
think of all those "singin' in the rain" friends. They are
a true gift!

A Wealthy Girl

When finances are tight or economic conditions are bleak, we are still rich as long as we have our girlfriends around. You, my friend, make me feel very rich indeed. . .even when my pocketbook is empty!

Strategic Friendships

Father, sometimes I wonder what my life would be like without the people You have so strategically placed around me. Then I'm grateful that I only have to wonder. Thank You so much for giving me just the right friends!

A Friend's Help

It is not so much our friends' help that helps us as the confident knowledge that they will help us.

EPICURUS

Stormy Weather

Sometimes we go through rough patches with our friends, even our best friends. Thank goodness we serve a forgiving God who shows us how to love and forgive each other. If you've been going through a rough patch, may today be a day of healing between you and your friend.

The Extra Mile

Have you ever had a girlfriend who went the extra mile for you—who was always there, even when others didn't show up? A friend who goes the extra mile is a friend indeed! And she deserves the same generous response from you when she is in need!

Friends to the Rescue!

Lord, sometimes I get overwhelmed by life.
Then You send a good friend to the rescue.
She pours herself out on my behalf. She gives
freely of herself, her time, and her resources.
I've done nothing to deserve such kindness,
but oh, I'm so grateful!

Together in the Darkness

Walking with a friend in the dark is better than
walking alone in the light.

HELEN KELLER

Salad Bar

Hanging out with a large group of girlfriends is like visiting the salad bar. You can load your plate with a variety of goodies. They are all different. . .in taste, texture, and appearance. Oh, but when you join them all together, what a delicious meal!

Heart Prints

Many people will walk in and out of your life, but only
true friends will leave footprints on your heart.

ANONYMOUS

An Eclectic Group

Father, sometimes I look at my group of
girlfriends and marvel at how different we are.
How fun to think that You merged such an eclectic
group. We have so much to learn from each
other. . .and so much to give. Thank You for my
"salad bowl" of friends!

Anybody Up?

It's the ones you can call up at 4:00 a.m. that really matter.

MARLENE DIETRICH

Heard It through the Grapevine

Girlfriends like to gossip. It's true. Even Christian friends sometimes slip into this trap. The "juicy tidbits" make for fun chatter, though sometimes at the expense of others. Why not proclaim today a gossip-free day? Commit to talking *to* your friends, not about them.

In a Good Light

Don't you love it when people think about you in a good light? Friends who know you—really know you—know the motives of your heart. They think the best of you. Aren't you grateful for friends like that?

A Guarded Tongue

Father, sometimes I really need Your help guarding
my tongue. I get together with my friends and
we just start talking. We don't mean to gossip,
but sometimes we do it anyway.
Help me in this area, Lord.

Different Paths

We all take different paths in life, but no matter where
we go, we take a little of each other everywhere.

TIM MCGRAW

What to Wear

The Bible instructs us to put on kindness, compassion, gentleness, patience, and self-control. What a classy ensemble! When we dress for success, we are wonderful friends to those in our sphere of influence. Praise the Lord for a great wardrobe!

Listen to the Silence

Everyone hears what you say. Friends listen to what
you say. Best friends listen to what you don't say.

ANONYMOUS

Fools Rush In

We all tend to be a little impulsive at times, don't
we? Aren't you glad the Lord has placed friends
in your life who keep you from making rash
decisions? Sometimes our girlfriends are just the
safety net we need.

Love Never Fails

Love is patient, love is kind. It does not envy, it does not boast, it is not proud. It is not rude, it is not self-seeking, it is not easily angered, it keeps no record of wrongs. Love does not delight in evil but rejoices with the truth. It always protects, always trusts, always hopes, always perseveres. Love never fails.

1 CORINTHIANS 13:4–8 NIV

A Greater Work

Lord, You've done a great work in my friends's life already. I pray now that You would bring confidence to replace doubt, peace to replace pain, and strength to replace weariness, and joy to replace sorrow. Work through her as never before, Father.

Bearing Burdens

The world can be a "weighty" place. Twenty-first-century women carry so many responsibilities. Who can help us shoulder some of the burden? Our girlfriends, of course. Today, spend some time thanking the Lord for your burden-bearing friends!

Blessings for You

May there always be work for your hands to do;
May your purse always hold a coin or two.
May the sun always shine on your windowpane;
May a rainbow be certain to follow each rain.
May the hand of a friend always be near you;
May God fill your heart with gladness to cheer you.

IRISH BLESSING

Through Laughter
and Tears

Lord, I treasure every tear shed with a friend. I also treasure the joyful moments, when laughter gets the best of us. Thank You, Father, for such precious memories with someone who means so very much to me!

The World Is a Garden

The world is so empty if one thinks only of mountains,
rivers, and cities; but to know someone here and there
who thinks and feels with us, and though distant,
is close to us in spirit, this makes the earth for us
an inhabited garden.

JOHANN WOLFGANG VON GOETHE

Get Over It

Ever feel like telling someone to "just get over it"?
Sometimes we need to give ourselves that advice,
don't we? Our feelings get hurt so easily. Thank
goodness for friends who can, in their own loving way,
help us get over the tough things.

Old Friends

Two may talk together under the same roof for
many years, yet never really meet; and two others
at first speech are old friends.

MARY CATHERWOOD

Simple Things

Father, I love the simple things in life—laughing with a good friend, sharing a meal, watching a funny movie. Thank You for the privilege of sharing life's simple joys with the good friends You've placed in my life.

The Holly Tree

Love is like the wild-rose briar;
Friendship is like the holly-tree.
The holly is dark when the rose briar blooms,
But which will bloom most constantly?

EMILY BRONTË

The Privilege of Friendship

What a delightful privilege to enter into relationship with a sister in Christ. I count it both an honor and a joy to share in your life, my sister, my friend. Truly we are kindred spirits.

Love One Another

"A new command I give you: Love one another.
As I have loved you, so you must love one another.
By this all men will know that you are my disciples,
if you love one another."

JOHN 13:34–35 NIV

Learning to Love

Lord, I'm just discovering what it means to truly love. You're teaching me to love You, to love others, and to love myself. Thank You for placing wonderful girlfriends in my life. They, too, teach me how to love.

Walk beside Me

Don't walk in front of me; I may not follow. Don't
walk behind me; I may not lead. Walk beside me and
be my friend.

ALBERT CAMUS

Mustard-Seed Faith

A good friend is the best sort of encourager.
She knows how to water my tiny mustard seed of faith
and make it grow. In doing so, she reminds me that my
situation is filled with hope.

Strong. . .for a Reason

We who are strong ought to bear with the failings
of the weak and not to please ourselves. Each of us
should please his neighbor for his good,
to build him up.

ROMANS 15:1–2 NIV

Encouragers

Lord, when I look at the word *encourage*, I realize that
encouragers are people who boost my courage.
When my girlfriends support me, I feel invincible.
Thank You for sending such great encouragers, Lord.
They truly give me courage to fight life's battles.

Laughter and Tears

Laugh and the world laughs with you. Cry and you cry
with your girlfriends.

LAURIE KUSLANSKY

Decorating Divas

Girlfriends decorate our lives. They add sparkle and shine, glitz and glam. And talk about makeover artists! They know when we're due for a change and expertly guide us through those changes every step of the way.

Being Me

If you're alone, I'll be your shadow. If you want to
cry, I'll be your shoulder. If you want a hug, I'll be
your pillow. If you need to be happy, I'll be your
smile. But anytime you need a friend,
I'll just be me.

UNKNOWN

A Diamond

You, my friend, are a precious diamond, a rare jewel.
You have taught me to dig deep to find life's real
gems. Your value is immeasurable, your "shimmer"
unparalleled. Best of all, you are a genuine reflection
of our Creator God. He shines through you.

Knowing You
Believe in Me

The glory of friendship is not in the outstretched hand, nor the kindly smile, nor the joy of companionship; it is in the spiritual inspiration that comes to one when he discovers that someone else believes in him and is willing to trust him.

RALPH WALDO EMERSON

Fruit of the Spirit

But the fruit of the Spirit is love, joy, peace,
longsuffering, gentleness, goodness, faith, meekness,
temperance: against such there is no law.

GALATIANS 5:22–23 KJV

Fruity Friends

Lord, I thank You for friends who exhibit the fruit
of the Spirit. Their "fruity" lifestyle encourages
me as I see them radiate peace and love. I long to
emulate their patience, gentleness, goodness,
and faith. And the joy they exude puts a
smile on every face.

Loving Speeches

Do not save your loving speeches for your friends till
they are dead. Do not write them on their tombstones;
speak them rather now instead.

ANNA CUMMINS

A Good Egg

A true friend is one who thinks you are a good egg
even if you are half-cracked.

UNKNOWN

The Song in My Heart

A friend knows the song in my heart and sings it to me
when my memory fails.

DONNA ROBERTS

Makeup

Women use makeup to cover up everything from blemishes to freckles to scars. We don't like "the real us" to show through, for fear people won't like what they see. Thank goodness for girlfriends who are comfortable with letting others see their flaws!

Greater Things

The Lord has already done many great things in your life, my friend. He has accomplished much through you. However, I believe even greater things lie ahead. My prayer for you is that all of your tomorrows will be even better than your yesterdays.

The Knowledge of Friendship

In loneliness, in sickness, in confusion—the mere
knowledge of friendship makes it possible to endure,
even if the friend is powerless to help. It is enough that
they exist. Friendship is not diminished by distance or
time, by imprisonment or war, by suffering or silence.
It is in these things that it roots most deeply. It is from
these things that it flowers.

PAM BROWN

A Day of Blessings

Lord, I pray that today will be a day of blessings for
my friend. May she feel Your presence in all she does,
whether it be work or play. And may she know the love
of all those with whom she comes in contact.

One Dear Friend

There is one friend in the life of each of us who
seems not a separate person, however dear and
beloved, but an expansion, an interpretation,
of one's self, the very meaning of one's soul.

EDITH WHARTON

Cry Me a River

Some of us are weepier than others. We cry at the
drop of a hat. We need friends who can handle our
occasional emotional outbursts. Thank you for being
the kind of friend who lets me spill a few tears on your
shoulder when I'm blue.

Insight in All Things

Think over these things I am saying [understand them and grasp their application], for the Lord will grant you full insight and understanding in everything.

2 TIMOTHY 2:7 AMP

For My Friend

Lord, I ask that You reveal Yourself to my friend today as never before. Invigorate her with power from on high. Give her discernment to make the right decisions, and minister to her at the point of her deepest need.

Somewhere in the Middle

Yesterday brought the beginning, tomorrow brings
the end, but somewhere in the middle
we've become best of friends.

ANONYMOUS

We Can Work It Out

Even the best of friends have their points of
contention. Life would be dull if we all agreed on
everything, don't you think? Today I'm grateful for
friends who go the extra mile to work things out with
me, even when I'm off base!

The Measure of Friendship

Sometimes the measure of friendship isn't your ability to not harm but your capacity to forgive the things done to you and ask forgiveness for your own mistakes.

RANDY K. MILHOLLAND

Eyes to Behold You

O gracious and holy Father, give us wisdom to perceive You, intellect to understand You, diligence to seek You, patience to wait for You, eyes to behold You, a heart to meditate upon You, and a life to proclaim You; through the power of the Spirit of Jesus Christ our Lord.

PRAYER OF ST. BENEDICT

Mutual Caring

Friendship involves mutual caring. It's not one-sided. I care about you—your welfare, your concerns—and you care about me. Neither of us overwhelms the other. I'm so grateful for friends who don't insist on a lopsided friendship.

Think on These Things

Finally, brothers, whatever is true, whatever is noble, whatever is right, whatever is pure, whatever is lovely, whatever is admirable—if anything is excellent or praiseworthy—think about such things. Whatever you have learned or received or heard from me, or seen in me—put it into practice. And the God of peace will be with you.

PHILIPPIANS 4:8–9 NIV

Speaking the
Truth in Love

You are the kind of friend who can give it to me
straight. You can speak the truth in love, often sharing
things that are tough to hear. What an art. . .to be able
to share hard truth in a loving way.

The Best Conversation

The best kind of friend is the one you could sit on a porch with, never saying a word, and walk away feeling like that was the best conversation you've had.

UNKNOWN

Sweet Release

Father, thank You for giving me the ability to
forgive when others speak ill of me. Today, help
me release the pain of any negative words spoken
over me. I lay my hurt feelings at Your feet,
Father, and ask You for complete healing.

Level Paths

Make level paths for your feet and take only ways that are firm. Do not swerve to the right or the left; keep your foot from evil.

PROVERBS 4:26–27 NIV

Real Friend

You're the reason I never needed an imaginary friend.

ANONYMOUS

Side-by-Side Friendship

True friendship is when two friends can walk in
opposite directions, yet remain side by side.

ANONYMOUS

A Prayer for Relationships

Lord, I know that my friend has many
relationships with friends and family members—
some simple, others complicated. Today, would
You give her the tools she needs to make those
relationships the very best they can be?

Precious Jewels

Among life's precious jewels,
Genuine and rare,
The one that we call friendship
Has worth beyond compare.

UNKNOWN

Handbags

We girls love our handbags, don't we? We stuff them
full of things we need. . .and things we don't.
Have you ever considered the fact that we carry
around a lot of excess emotional baggage, too? Today,
offer that baggage to the Lord.

Blossoming Friendship

The most beautiful discovery true friends make is that
they can grow separately without growing apart.

ELISABETH FOLEY

Financial Blessing

Thank You, Lord, for meeting all of my friend's
financial needs. She has cried out to You for so
many things over the years. Remind her today that
You will never leave her or forsake her. Give her
the confidence to know that she can prosper as her
soul prospers!

Pluses and Minuses

I'm treating you as a friend, asking you to share my
present minuses in the hope that I can ask you to share
my future pluses.

KATHERINE MANSFIELD

The Balm of Gilead

My prayer for you today, my friend, is for peace. . .
in the middle of the storm, in the midst of the chaos.
Peace. May the Balm of Gilead soothe your troubled
soul and bring calm reassurance.

Comforted and Edified

Wherefore comfort yourselves together, and edify
one another, even as also ye do.

1 THESSALONIANS 5:11 KJV

Speak to Me

Lord, You speak into my life through so many
different people—my pastor, my spouse,
my children, my parents. Thank You that You also
choose to speak to me through my girlfriends.
May my ears always be attuned to Your voice,
no matter whom You speak through.

Friendship Is. . .

Friendship is a comforting smile, a familiar voice that warms the heart, and the freedom to be the person God intended.

ANONYMOUS

My Favorite Things

If I were to list my favorite things in the world—Rocky Road ice cream, kittens, the smell of a baby after her bath—I would place you high on the list. You, my friend, are truly one of my "favorite things."

Make Me Worthy

Since it has been my lot to find,
At every parting of the road,
The helping hand of comrade kind
To help me with my heavy load,
And since I have no gold to give
And love alone must make amends,
My humble prayer is, while I live—
God, make me worthy of my friends.

ANONYMOUS

Fun-Loving Friendships

Lord, thank You for silly friends—the ones
who aren't afraid to be laughed at. They giggle
and snort. . .and generally make a scene. I'm so
grateful You've lightened my load by sending these
fun-loving women into my life!

Mirror Image

The only service a friend can really render is to keep up your courage by holding up to you a mirror in which you can see a noble image of yourself.

GEORGE BERNARD SHAW

Worship in Spirit and Truth

Oh Lord, thank You for giving me a worshipper's heart. There is no higher calling than to praise the Creator of the universe. I'm honored that You've sent like-minded friends. May we, together, always worship You in Spirit and in truth.

The Best Light

Treat your friends as you do your pictures, and place them in their best light.

JENNIE JEROME CHURCHILL

Established

Almighty God, Father of our Lord Jesus Christ,
establish and confirm us in Your truth by Your
Holy Spirit. Reveal to us what we do not know;
perfect in us what is lacking; strengthen us in what
we know; and keep us faultless in Your service;
through the same Jesus Christ our Lord.

PRAYER OF
CLEMENT OF ROME

Born of God

Beloved, let us love one another: for love is of God; and
every one that loveth is born of God, and knoweth God.

1 JOHN 4:7 KJV

Let the Son Shine

The light of Jesus shines brightly through our actions,
our worship, and our study of the Word. It also shines
in our relationships with friends. What a "shiny"
blessing you are, my sweet friend. You are a reflection
of His great light.

Great Friends

Truly great friends are hard to find, difficult to leave,
and impossible to forget.

ANONYMOUS

Lighting the Way

Father, I thank You for friends who reflect You.
They don't have to preach or teach; the light that
radiates from them is lesson enough. Lord, may I
truly be a reflection of You so that I can light the
way for others.

An Interpretation of the World

Our friends interpret the world and ourselves to us,
if we take them tenderly and truly.

AMOS BRONSON ALCOTT

Interrupted!

Okay, admit it: Sometimes your friends show up at the most inopportune times, don't they? You're right in the middle of dealing with something tough and your doorbell rings. Instead of groaning, look at these "interruptions" as divine appointments, for that is what they are!

Ships, Ships, and More Ships

There are many types of ships. There are wooden ships, plastic ships, and metal ships. But the best and most important types of ships are friendships.

OLD IRISH QUOTE

A Garden of Friendship

Lord, my friends are like flowers in the garden of
my life. They add color, fragrance,
and beauty. You've arranged them in colorful array,
each one different from the others. I love them
individually. . .and together as a beautiful bouquet.

The Evidence

One of the surest evidences of friendship that one individual can display to another is telling him gently of a fault. If any other can excel it, it is listening to such a disclosure with gratitude, and amending the error.

EDWARD G. BULWER-LYTTON

Moody Me

Ah, moods. Who can predict them? One minute
they're up; the next they're down. They seem to change
like the weather. I'm so glad I have girlfriends who
understand—and put up with—my varying moods.
God bless them for their patience!

Pure Joy

Consider it pure joy, my brothers, whenever you face
trials of many kinds, because you know that the testing
of your faith develops perseverance. Perseverance
must finish its work so that you may be mature and
complete, not lacking anything.

JAMES 1:2–4 NIV

Family Ties

Father, I'm so grateful for the body of Christ—
my family. Though we are vastly different, we are
still Your children. I'm especially thankful for
my sisters in the Lord. We are truly like siblings,
in nearly every sense of the word.

A Blessing for My Friend

The LORD bless thee, and keep thee: The LORD make his face shine upon thee, and be gracious unto thee: The LORD lift up his countenance upon thee, and give thee peace.

NUMBERS 6:24–26 KJV

The Treasure of Friendship

A friend is a treasure
More precious than gold,
For love shared is priceless
And never grows old.

ANONYMOUS

Cleaning Up after Me

Sometimes friendships get a little messy. One person erupts and leaves a mess for the other to clean up. Thanks to all of the girlfriends who've cleaned up after me over the years. You can count on me to return the favor!

A Healthy Supplement

Friendship is like vitamins; we supplement each
other's minimum daily requirements.

ANONYMOUS

Invigorating Friendship

Father, I get so weary sometimes. I wake up, race through the day, do the work of three people, then tumble into bed at night. Just about the time I think I can't keep going, You send a friend to invigorate me with her positive, uplifting attitude. Bless You, Lord!

Glad Hearts

A friendship that's sincere and true
Gives joy like nothing else will do;
That's why glad hearts look up and send
A prayer of thanks for faithful friends.

ANONYMOUS

Send in the Clowns

I get way too serious sometimes. Life doesn't leave much room for silliness. Praise the Lord for friends who know how—and when—to interrupt my seriousness with a little fun. Their clowning around isn't irreverent; on the contrary, it is often a lifesaver!

Return to Me

It's funny how, in the end, you always go back to
the ones who were there from the beginning.

ANONYMOUS

All Things New

Wonderful Creator, You make all things new.
I'm grateful for all of the new friendships You've
brought my way in recent years. And I love how You've
taken my "old" friendships and made them even
stronger!

Never Forsaken

"Be strong and courageous. Do not be afraid or terrified because of them, for the LORD your God goes with you; he will never leave you nor forsake you."

DEUTERONOMY 31:6 NIV

Nourishment

I am a big believer that you have to nourish any relationship. I am still very much a part of my friends' lives and they are very much a part of my life. A First Lady who does not have this source of strength and comfort can lose perspective and become isolated.

NANCY REAGAN

Looking Back

We always thought we'd look back on our tears and laugh, but we never thought we'd look back on our laughter and cry.

UNKNOWN

A Burst of Creativity

Lord, would You bless my friend with creativity and
inspiration today? Give her fresh ideas and a renewed
sense of purpose. Remind her that You have called her
to do spectacular things for You. Anoint her for the
tasks ahead.

Your Corner of the Forest

You can't stay in your corner of the Forest waiting for others to come to you. You have to go to them sometimes.

FROM *POOH'S LITTLE INSTRUCTION BOOK*,
INSPIRED BY A. A. MILNE

Coaxing

Have you ever had to coax a friend out of her
shyness? Perhaps you're the shy one, needing a bit
of encouragement from a friend. How wonderful to
have friends who can coax us to be the best we can
be without hurting our feelings or making us feel
insecure.

Heartsong

A friend is someone who knows the song in your heart and can sing it back to you when you have forgotten the words.

ANONYMOUS

God Pleaser

Lord, my friend needs Your touch today. She's trying so hard to please so many people. She wants to be everything to everyone, but I see the weariness in her eyes. Today, remind her that the only One she really needs to please is You.

Eternal Friendships

Isn't it amazing to think about the fact that we're
not just going to be friends in this lifetime—we'll be
spending eternity together! The joys we experience
here on earth are just a foretaste of the extraordinary
adventures that lie ahead!

A Reminder Not to Be Afraid

"So do not fear, for I am with you; do not be dismayed, for I am your God. I will strengthen you and help you; I will uphold you with my righteous right hand."

ISAIAH 41:10 NIV

The Company You Keep

We're known by the company we keep. . .or so the
saying goes. With such a wide array friends, I must
be known for my diversity! What about you—
whose company do you keep? Who—or what—
are you "known" for?

Double My Joy

I'm so grateful for you, my friend. So many times you have doubled my joy and divided my grief. You're always there to rejoice with me when times are good, and you're just as willing to cry with me when times are bad.

Bacon Bits

Friends are the bacon bits in the salad bowl of life.

PIZZA PLACE SIGN

Amazing Grace

When I spend time with my girlfriends, I am reminded of God's amazing grace. They are a reflection of His heart for me—overflowing with graciousness and goodness. Today, my wish for you is that you would experience the Lord's amazing grace in your life.

Choose You This Day

We have to be careful with the choices we make,
especially when it comes to friends. After all,
we tend to become like the people we hang out
with. Having godly girlfriends is the best! Their
focus on the Lord is inspiring, and they're
a blast to be around!

Letting Go

Father, sometimes I let the bites and stings from angry words hurt me. I hang on to things when I should be letting go. Today, I release those hurts I've been holding on to. Heal any broken friendships. Soften our hearts so that we can walk in restored relationship.

Sticks and Stones

Sticks and stones are hard on bones
Aimed with angry art;
Words can sting like anything
But silence breaks the heart.

SUZANNE NICHOLS

True Colors

You know what I love best about you,
my friend? You are who you say you are. You're
not pretending to be something—or someone—
you're not. Thanks for letting your true colors
shine through. What a great testimony!

True Friendship

True friendship is like sound health;
the value of it is seldom known until it be lost.

CHARLES CALEB COLTON

Acceptance

Father, it's such a relief that I can be myself around my
girlfriends and they will accept me anyway. Knowing
I'm loved and accepted means so much. But even when
others don't accept me, Lord, I'm grateful that You do.
I can never escape from Your love.

Living in Harmony

Finally, all of you, live in harmony with one another;
be sympathetic, love as brothers, be compassionate
and humble. Do not repay evil with evil or insult with
insult, but with blessing, because to this you were
called so that you may inherit a blessing.

1 PETER 3:8–9 NIV

A Circle of Trust

Jesus had a tight-knit circle of friends. They leaned on each other and offered support as He ministered to people. We operate best in these small groups. I'm so glad you're in mine. . .and I'm in yours!

Every Day a Holiday!

Celebrate the happiness that friends are
always giving, make every day a holiday,
and celebrate just living.

AMANDA BRADLEY

A Force to Be
Reckoned With

Lord, give us eyes to see others around the globe as
You see them. Show me how I can link arms with my
friends to make a difference for those who are hurting.
May we be a force to be reckoned with!

Troubled Wings

Friends are angels who lift our feet when our own
wings have trouble remembering how to fly.

ANONYMOUS

I've Got the Joy!

Remember that song you used to sing as a child about having the joy, joy, joy, joy down in your heart? Today, I pray that you may come in contact with joy givers. . .and with those who are in need of a dose of the joy you have to give.

Footprints on the Heart

Some people come into our lives and quickly
go. Some people move our souls to dance. They
awaken us to new understanding with the passing
whisper of their wisdom. Some people make the
sky more beautiful to gaze upon. They stay in our
lives for a while, leave footprints on our hearts,
and we are never ever the same.

FLAVIA WEEDN

The Innermost Places

Lord, where would I be without friends who've allowed
me into the innermost places of their hearts?
Surely we are bonded because we've touched each other
in such deep ways. What a beautiful revelation of trust.

Keeping Watch

Watch your thoughts; they become words.
Watch your words; they become actions.
Watch your actions; they become habits.
Watch your habits; they become character.
Watch your character, for it becomes your destiny!

ANONYMOUS

Stuck in the Middle
with You

Do you ever feel stuck. . .like you can't go forward and can't go back? Sometimes it's hard to know what to do, which decision to make. Thank goodness for girlfriends who are willing to spend time helping us sort things out when we're stuck!

Never Afraid

The LORD is my light and my salvation—whom
shall I fear? The LORD is the stronghold of my
life—of whom shall I be afraid?

PSALM 27:1 NIV

Frozen

Sometimes, Lord, I feel frozen in place. I need someone
to come along and thaw me out so that I can move
forward. Father, You're so good to send my friends to
help me out of those "frozen" places. They provide just
the right amount of warmth to get me going!

Advice

Advice is like snow; the softer it falls, the longer it
dwells upon, and the deeper it sinks into, the mind.

SAMUEL TAYLOR COLERIDGE

Popcorn and a Movie

When you hear the words "popcorn and a movie," what comes to mind? Likely, your girlfriends! How relaxing to watch a great chick flick with your best friends. Talk about the perfect evening!

By Your Side

If looking back hurts you and looking forward
scares you, then look to your side and
I'll always be there.

ANONYMOUS

Cultivating Friendship

My dear friend, thank you for caring for me as you
would tend to a plant, watering me when the need
arises and cultivating me so I can be the very best I can
be. I will return the favor so that, together,
we can blossom and grow.

Are You Listening?

If the person you are talking to doesn't appear to be
listening, be patient. It may simply be that he has a
small piece of fluff in his ear.

FROM *POOH'S LITTLE INSTRUCTION BOOK*,
INSPIRED BY A. A. MILNE

Happy Days

My days are happier now that you're in them, my sweet
friend. In fact, I can scarcely remember what life was
like before I knew you. Could it have been this sweet?
Surely not! I thank God every day for the happiness
you bring.

A Hundred Minus One Day

If you live to be a hundred, I want to live to be a hundred minus one day, so I never have to live without you.

WINNIE-THE-POOH

Answered Prayers

Thank You, Lord, that You both hear and answer our prayers. Today my friend has several requests to lay at Your feet. Give her Your answers for her problems, Lord. May she be reminded that You hear. . .and respond.

Bold and Confident

I write these things to you who believe in the name of the Son of God so that you may know that you have eternal life. This is the confidence we have in approaching God: that if we ask anything according to his will, he hears us. And if we know that he hears us—whatever we ask—we know that we have what we asked of him.

1 JOHN 5:13–15 NIV

Shopping Extravaganza

Few things are more enjoyable than shopping with a girlfriend. She makes a day at the mall so much fun. Even when there's no money to spend, it's still great fun to window-shop with a like-minded sister. I'm so thankful for my "shop till you drop" girlfriends!

Challenging Each Other

Isn't it great to have edifying friendships?
The kind that push you toward God's purposes and
calling in your life? We women love a challenge,
and having girlfriends who challenge us in this
way is a real bonus!

A Friend in Need

Father, my heart is heavy when I think about my friends who are hurting. Today, I ask that You reach down and wipe away every tear. Cradle my friends in Your loving arms and gently console them as only You can.

Hand in Hand

Remember, we all stumble, every one of us. That's why it's a comfort to go hand in hand.

EMILY KIMBROUGH

Me? Off Track?

Sometimes I overreact or get off track. Sometimes I come up with goofy ideas. Still, you always smile and encourage me. Thank you, my friend, for not telling me what a goofball you think I am. You're such a blessing!

Icing on the Cake

Girlfriends are like icing on the cake of life.
They are that added sweetness we don't really
deserve but we're glad to have anyway! Best of all,
they don't add any calories. Thank you for the
sweetness you add to my life, my friend.

Crooked Places Straight

I'm grateful to you, my friend, for helping me make the crooked places in my life straight. You keep me from veering off too far to the right or left. I appreciate your gentle intervention during "off" seasons, as well as your ongoing encouragement.

Trusting God

Four things to learn in life:
To think clearly without hurry or confusion;
To love everybody sincerely;
To act in everything with the highest motives;
To trust God unhesitatingly.

HELEN KELLER

Attitude Check

Lord, sometimes I need an attitude check. I get a little cranky. I'm grateful You deal with my crankiness in a gentle way, and I'm glad to have friends who do, too! Thanks for Your patience, Lord!

Waiting on the Lord

Why are you in despair, O my soul? And why have
you become disturbed within me? Hope in God,
for I shall again praise Him for the help of
His presence.

PSALM 42:5 NASB

Thank Goodness for Love!

A crowd is not company, faces are but a gallery of pictures, and talk but a tinkling cymbal, where there is no love.

FRANCIS BACON

Sunlight on the Heart

A friend is like sunlight, filtering into the quiet
corners of one's heart, offering bright new mornings
and fresh hope yet demanding nothing in return.

ANONYMOUS

Comfortable Silence

Oh, my dear friend! I'm so happy to share times of comfortable silence with you. Neither has to say a word, and yet we know each other's deepest thoughts. What a blessing to hear in the silence.

A Noble Undertaking

To have a good friend is one of the highest
delights in life; to be a good friend is one of the
noblest and most difficult undertakings.

ANONYMOUS

Facing Our Goliaths

Lord, please give my friend courage today to face the
Goliaths in her life. She needs Your reassurance and
Your mighty power. Show me how I can be the sort of
friend she needs to help her face life's challenges.

Free-Flowing Friendship

Friendship that flows from the heart cannot be frozen
by adversity, as the water that flows from the spring
cannot congeal in winter.

JAMES FENIMORE COOPER

Summer Breeze

Friendship is like a wonderful breeze in the summertime. It provides just exactly what you need when you need it. Thank you for "blowing" through my life, my sweet friend. I so enjoy the refreshment of your presence.

A Tight Squeeze

A good friend—like a tube of toothpaste—
comes through in a tight squeeze.

ANNONYMOUS

Friends from
Days Gone By

Lord, please be with all of those dear friends I rarely
get to see anymore—the ones I used to be so close to.
Whisper words of love to them and let them know they
are not forgotten.

Mutual Faith

For I long to see you, that I may impart to you some
spiritual gift, so that you may be established—that
is, that I may be encouraged together with you by the
mutual faith both of you and me.

ROMANS 1:11–12 NKJV

Forever Friends

You are a "forever" friend—the sort of friend I hope to
have with me from now until we meet again in heaven.
Forever friends don't give up when times get tough.
They work their way through difficult situations.
Thanks for sticking with me, my friend!

Joy Partners

Every man rejoices twice when he has a partner
in his joy. He who shares tears with us wipes them
away. He divides them in two, and he who laughs
with us makes the joy double.

FULTON J. SHEEN

True Beauty

Thank You, Lord, that we are all beautiful in Your sight. I don't have to rely on the world to tell me what true beauty is. I know what it is because I recognize it every time I look into the face of one of my friends.

Unexplainable Friendship

Friendship is the hardest thing in the world to explain. It's not something you can be taught in school, but if you haven't learned the value of friendship, you haven't really learned anything at all.

MUHAMMAD ALI

He's Got the Whole World in His Hands

We serve a big God who loves people of all different shapes, sizes, colors, and races. He doesn't discriminate. I love the fact that our friendship isn't bound by outward appearance. When you look at people, you simply see them as God's children.

Hand-Holding Friends

The friend who holds your hand and says the
wrong thing is made of dearer stuff than the one
who stays away.

BARBARA KINGSOLVER

The Giver of Gifts

Lord, You are the giver of gifts. You're constantly pouring out Your blessings lavishly. Perhaps one of the greatest gifts You've ever given me are my girlfriends. Each package is unique, but together they make every day feel like Christmas.

Attitude Is Everything

A happy person is not a person in a certain set of circumstances, but rather a person with a certain set of attitudes.

HUGH DOWNS

Give Her a Hand!

The Bible teaches that Eve was taken from Adam's rib.
Wonder where a best friend comes from?
She must be taken from my hand. She's always there,
hand extended, to lift me up when I've fallen.
Her hands are folded together in prayer just
when I need it.

May You Prosper

Dear friend, I pray that you may enjoy good health
and that all may go well with you, even as your soul
is getting along well.

3 JOHN 1:2 NIV

The Richest Girl

Lord, I feel like the richest girl on the planet when I consider my girlfriends. They add tremendous value to my life. I would sooner have my friends than all the riches the world could bring.

The Sunshine of Life

Friendship is precious, not only in the shade, but in the sunshine of life; and thanks to a benevolent arrangement of things, the greater part of life is sunshine.

THOMAS JEFFERSON

Safety

My friend, may we always feel as safe around each other as we do right now. May our words never sting, our expressions never injure, and our actions never cause pain. Thank you for making me feel so protected.

Built Up in Faith

But you, dear friends, build yourselves up in your
most holy faith and pray in the Holy Spirit.
Keep yourselves in God's love as you wait for
the mercy of our Lord Jesus Christ to bring
you to eternal life.

JUDE 1:20–21 NIV

Greater Intimacy

Father, I long to grow closer to You. I know my girlfriends desire that, too. We ask for a renewal, Lord. Where there is spiritual stagnation, stir us up. When we feel separated from you, please reveal Your nearness. Draw us into greater intimacy with You.

Five Real Friends

My father always used to say that when you die,
if you've got five real friends, then you've had a great life.

LEE IACOCCA

No Distance Too Great

Aren't you glad that distance doesn't matter in friendship? Even if we're miles away, we're still as close as our next heartbeat. Closeness is a matter of caring, not a matter of miles. Thank you for being my close friend!

Kindred Spirit

A bosom friend—an intimate friend, you
know—a really kindred spirit to whom I can
confide my inmost soul.

FROM *ANNE OF GREEN GABLES*
BY LUCY MAUD MONTGOMERY

Memories

Lord, the memories of the hours I've spent with my friends are precious to me. Sometimes I think about the laughter we've shared. . .the funny stories. . .and I can't help but chuckle. Other times I'm reminded of the quiet, sweet times and I'm overwhelmed with love.

My Friend. . .
God's Temple

Don't you know that you yourselves are God's temple
and that God's Spirit lives in you?

1 CORINTHIANS 3:16 NIV

Pass the Tissues

Talk about making yourself vulnerable! Almost
nothing makes you feel more vulnerable than having
a cry-fest with a girlfriend. Whether you're dealing
with a broken heart, clearing up a misunderstanding,
or shedding tears of happiness, there's no sweeter thing
than two friends sharing a box of tissues.

Intimate with a Few

Be courteous to all, but intimate with few,
and let those few be well tried before you give
them your confidence. True friendship is a plant
of slow growth, and must undergo and withstand
the shocks of adversity before it is entitled to
the appellation.

GEORGE WASHINGTON

Habits

Lord, some of my habits aren't so good; I need to deal with those. However, there's one habit I'm glad I don't have to change. I'm in the habit of meeting with my girlfriends for a time of worship and study. What a happy habit!

The Spark of Friendship

To cement a new friendship, especially between
foreigners or persons of a different social world,
a spark with which both were secretly charged must fly
from person to person, and cut across the accidents of
place and time.

CORNELIA OTIS SKINNER

Girl-Talk

Girlfriends are great when it comes to talking us through issues we face with the opposite sex. They help put things in perspective. There's always the giggly girl-talk, coupled with the occasional "that's a man thing" talk, but it's all in good fun. Girls. . .talking about boys? Of course!

Free to Be Me

Friends are life's finest blessings. *Friend* and *free* are from the same root word, perhaps because you are free to be yourself with a friend.

UNKNOWN

The Opposite Sex

Lord, whenever I face issues related to the man in my life (or lack thereof), I know I can count on my girlfriends to keep me sane. Thank You for using my friends to bring insight and balance regarding the opposite sex.

Reputation. . .
or Character?

Reputation is what men and women think of us;
character is what God and angels know of us.

THOMAS PAINE

Caring and Sharing

My friend, you are so generous. Your willingness to give comes from a heart of deep caring. I know you would give me the shirt off your back if I needed it. Thank you for giving of yourself so generously. My heart is full to bursting!

Pray for Each Other

Therefore confess your sins to each other and pray for each other so that you may be healed. The prayer of a righteous man is powerful and effective.

JAMES 5:16 NIV

Fight the Good Fight

Sometimes we need to fight our way through tough
situations, even when we're tempted to give up.
My prayer for you today, my friend, is that you will
keep fighting. Keep on keepin' on. Don't give up.
Don't give in. Fight the good fight.

Thinking of You

You know that place between asleep and awake?
Where you still remember dreaming? That's where I
will always think of you.

TINKERBELL

King's Kids

We're King's kids. Think about that for a moment.
We are daughters of the Most High God, and He
welcomes us into His inner courts. Private time with
the King of kings! Can you even imagine it? It's true.
Just one perk of having the ultimate Daddy.

A Time for Silence

Sometimes being a friend means mastering the art of timing. There is a time for silence. A time to let go and allow people to hurl themselves into their own destiny. And a time to prepare to pick up the pieces when it's all over.

OCTAVIA BUTLER

Jumping through Hoops

Thank You, Lord, that we don't have to earn Your love.
We don't have to jump through hoops to make You
happy. I ask that You remind my friend of this truth
today. Help her to relax and see that she is precious to
You no matter how much—or how little—she does.

What Bonds Us?

The bond that links your true family is not one of blood, but of respect and joy in each other's life. Rarely do members of one family grow up under the same roof.

RICHARD BACH

Silver and Gold

There's an old song that talks about making new friends but keeping the old; the former are silver, but the latter are gold. Today, spend a little time praising God for both your recent friends and the lifelong ones.

Faithful Friends

There are those who pass like ships in the night,
who meet for a moment, then sail out of sight
with never a backward glance of regret; folks we
know briefly then quickly forget. Then there are
friends who sail together, through quiet waters and
stormy weather, helping each other through joy
and through strife. And they are the kind who give
meaning to life.

UNKNOWN

Wholly Yours

Lord, today I praise You because You are worthy of praise. You've covered me with Your love and reminded me that I'm Your child. How wonderful to hear You call me Yours! I am a daughter of the risen Lord!

A Scripture for My Girlfriends

And my God will liberally supply (fill to the full) your every need according to His riches in glory in Christ Jesus.

PHILIPPIANS 4:19 AMP

Making Friends. . .a Gift!

Blessed are they who have the gift of making friends,
for it is one of God's best gifts. It involves many
things, but above all, the power of going out of one's
self and appreciating whatever is noble and loving in
another.

THOMAS HUGHES

Turn the World Around

Girlfriends are great at putting things in
perspective. When I'm fearful, they offer hope.
When I'm overly zealous, they rein me back in.
When things look bleak, they remind me of God's
promises. Isn't it great to have friends who help
you turn situations around?

A Prayer for Vision

Lord, today I ask that You bless my girlfriends who serve You. Help them to see their situations through Your eyes. May their spiritual vision be 20/20. Raise them up as leaders, Father, and encourage them in the faith.

A Gift from Above

When you ask God for a gift, be thankful if He sends
not diamonds, riches, or pearls, but the love of real
true friends.

ANONYMOUS

Jet-Setters

Wouldn't it be fun to travel the globe with a friend?
To hop in a jet and fly to Italy. . .or maybe Greece?
To take a cruise to the Caribbean? You are the sort of
friend I'd love to travel with. So let's start packing!

A Mountain-Moving God

I'm so grateful that You move mountains,
Lord. I'm facing a few, and I know my friends are,
too. Today, we choose to speak to them—in Your
mighty name—and watch them move. What a
relief to know we serve an all-powerful God!

Unchanging Friendship

A true friend unbosoms freely, advises justly, assists readily, adventures boldly, takes all patiently, defends courageously, and continues a friend unchangeably.

WILLIAM PENN

Rough Courage

I do not wish to treat friendships daintily, but with the roughest courage. When they are real, they are not glass threads or frost-work, but the solidest thing we know.

RALPH WALDO EMERSON

Take It to the Bank

You are my friend for life. You're not getting rid of me.
I plan to stick around through thick and thin,
good times and bad. You can take that news to the
bank, my friend. You're stuck with me!

Ask, Seek, and Knock

"Ask and it will be given to you; seek and you will
find; knock and the door will be opened to you.
For everyone who asks receives; he who seeks
finds; and to him who knocks,
the door will be opened."

MATTHEW 7:7–8 NIV

Starting Point

My friend, I pray that today will be a starting point
for a new adventure in your life. It's time to think big,
to pray for new things. Why not pause and do just
that. . .right now? Ask the Lord to make this day a
starting point.

Friends Like Walls

Friends are like walls. Sometimes you lean on them
and sometimes it is just enough to know they're there.

ANONYMOUS

While You're Waiting

Maybe you're waiting on something from the Lord. . .an answer to prayer, perhaps. While you're waiting, why not praise Him? Praising our Savior is a great way to spend your time, even if the answer seems a long time in coming.

Forgetful Friends

I've learned that people will forget what you said,
people will forget what you did, but people will
never forget how you made them feel.

MAYA ANGELOU

Letting Go

Lord, I desperately want peace in my life, but I've been stubborn! So many times I've tried to tell You how to be, God, thinking I had a better plan. Today I release my grip on my life so that You can do the work You long to do.

An Advance of Friendship

Never refuse any advance of friendship, for if nine out of ten bring you nothing, one alone may repay you.

MADAME DE TENCIN

Making Things Right

Ever have one of those days when absolutely
everything goes wrong? Then along comes a girlfriend,
and with a smile or a word, she makes it all right again.
Thank you for being such a friend.

Childlike Faith

Remember how carefree you were as a child?
You ran and played, never giving a thought to life's
cares. It's time to return to that simple childlike
faith, my friend. Today, take whatever is weighing
you down and offer it to your heavenly Father.

Open My Eyes, Lord

Lord, today I pray that You would open my eyes to see the needs in my friends' lives. May I not pass glibly by as they are hurting. Show me how to minister to the ones in need and how to encourage the ones who are in pain.

A Joyful Partnership

I thank my God every time I remember you. In all
my prayers for all of you, I always pray with joy because
of your partnership in the gospel from the first day
until now.

PHILIPPIANS 1:3–5 NIV

Living at Peace

There is really only one way to live at peace. It's not about garnering possessions or making more money. Peace comes with removing your hands from the reins of your life and giving God complete control. I pray that today will be a day of release for you.

Forgiven!

Just a reminder, my friend. . .God has forgiven you for the sins of the past. He has cast them as far as the east is from the west. Don't keep dredging up the failures of yesterday. God has let them go, and it's time for you to do the same!

All Profit

Talk is by far the most accessible of pleasures. It costs nothing in money, it is all profit, it completes our education, founds and fosters our friendships, and can be enjoyed at any age and in almost any state of health.

ROBERT LOUIS STEVENSON

Sugar and Spice

It's fun to have a girlfriend who adds both sugar and spice to our lives, isn't it? She knows when to sweeten the pot and when to add that little bit of "kick" to get us moving.

United in Laughter

A good laugh makes us better friends with ourselves
and everyone around us.

ORISON MARDEN

No Distance Too Great

Friends are always friends no matter how far you have to travel back in time. If you have memories together, there is always a piece of your friendship inside your heart.

KELLIE O'CONNOR

The Perfect Sacrifice

This is how God showed his love among us: He sent his one and only Son into the world that we might live through him. This is love: not that we loved God, but that he loved us and sent his Son as an atoning sacrifice for our sins.

1 JOHN 4:9–10 NIV

The Green-Eyed Monster

Lord, I have to confess that I sometimes get a little
jealous of my friends. It's not just their "stuff" that
makes me green with envy; it's the attention they get
from others. Lord, today I release any jealousies to You.

Stained Glass Windows

People are like stained glass windows. They sparkle
and shine when the sun is out, but when the darkness
sets in, their true beauty is revealed only if there is a
light from within.

ELISABETH KÜBLER-ROSS

Heavenly Addition

For this very reason, make every effort to add to
your faith goodness; and to goodness, knowledge;
and to knowledge, self-control; and to self-
control, perseverance; and to perseverance,
godliness; and to godliness, brotherly kindness;
and to brotherly kindness, love. For if you possess
these qualities in increasing measure, they will
keep you from being ineffective and unproductive
in your knowledge of our Lord Jesus Christ.

2 PETER 1:5–8 NIV

My Friend. . .a True Star

Friends are like stars. . .you don't always see them,
but you know they're always there.

HULALI LUTA

Politically Correct Friendship

Girlfriends don't always agree on everything, particularly when it comes to politics. Thank goodness our Christ-centered friendships can be "politically correct," even when we disagree. As long as we all vote for Jesus, we're on the same team!

There for You. . .Always

Thick and thin,
tall and small,
fast and slow.
Tell me who is always there for you.
I am sure you know.
Your best friend, of course;
don't let him or her go.

MATT MARKHAM

Riches Revealed

The greatest good you can do for another
is not just to share your riches but to reveal
to him his own.

BENJAMIN DISRAELI

The Girl in the Mirror

Lord, thank You that I don't have to be hung up on the reflection in the mirror. I know You see beyond that. Thank You for girlfriends who do, too. They see the real me, inside and out.

Taking the Bus

Lots of people want to ride with you in the limo,
but what you want is someone who will take the bus
with you when the limo breaks down.

OPRAH WINFREY

What? You, Too?

Friendship is born at that moment when one
person says to another, "What! You, too?
I thought I was the only one."

C. S. LEWIS

Deep Roots

My friend, would you like to know one of the
things I love most about you? Your roots.
No, not your hair. Your spiritual roots. They run
deep. . .and it shows. No wonder you stand so
strong and tall during life's storms.

Thought Life

Lord, we all struggle with our thoughts at one time or another. We allow ourselves to feel defeated. . .or we can't seem to forgive ourselves. Today, I give my thoughts to You, Father. Take them and free my mind to be wholly Yours.

Eternal Life

See that what you have heard from the beginning remains in you. If it does, you also will remain in the Son and in the Father. And this is what he promised us—even eternal life.

1 JOHN 2:24–25 NIV

Young at Heart

Only a really good friend can be trusted with a woman's real age. She will be the sort of friend who makes you feel fifteen, whether you're really sixty or seventy-five!

ANONYMOUS

Never-Ending Praise

Be joyful always; pray continually; give thanks in
all circumstances, for this is God's will for you in
Christ Jesus.

1 THESSALONIANS 5:16–18 NIV

Little-Girl Dreams

Remember when we were little girls, dreaming of being grown up? We pranced around in our mother's shoes, pretending. We thought it would never happen! Now, here we are. . .all grown up and doing great things for God. Look how far we've come!

A True Friend

A true friend is one who overlooks your failures and
tolerates your success!

DOUG LARSON

A Shield about Us

Lord, wrap Your arms like a cocoon around my friend today. May she sense Your closeness as never before. Shield her from the voices of the world and the discouragement of the enemy. Keep her safe in You.

My Friend. . .My World

A single rose can be my garden. . .
a single friend, my world.

LEO BUSCAGLIA

My Friends. . .My Family

The best part of life is when your family becomes your
friends, and your friends become your family.

DANICA WHITFIELD

A Fragrant Aroma

One of the most appealing things about our girlfriends is that they add a fragrant aroma to our lives. They are pleasant to be around and make us want to be better than we are. Today, praise the Lord for your "fragrant" friends.

Get Over Yourself!

A best friend knows when to tell you to get over
yourself and is one of the few who can get by with it.

ROBIN SURFACE KNOTT

High-Tech Friends

It's fun to be friends during such a high-tech generation. Text messages. E-mails. Goofy forwards. Facebook. MySpace. Blogs. We have a lot of fun keeping in touch, don't we? I love spending time with my high-tech friends!

Children of God

How great is the love the Father has lavished on us, that we should be called children of God! And that is what we are! The reason the world does not know us is that it did not know him.

1 JOHN 3:1 NIV

A Career Blessing

Lord, bless my friend in her career today. Give her all
the tools she needs to be truly successful in her field.
May she be a light to her coworkers and an example to
all who come in contact with her. Bless the work of her
hands, Father.

For Such a Time as This

Lord, I thank You that my girlfriends and I were born "for such a time as this." It's no accident that we're living in the twenty-first century. You've placed us here during this generation on purpose. . .so that we can reach others for You.

Oh, Those Changes

Women certainly know what it means to go through changes. Seems like every time we look in the mirror, our body is a little different from the day before. And talk about hormonal changes. Wowza! Thanks for sticking with me through the changes in my life!

What Faults?

Every man should have a fair-sized cemetery in which
to bury the faults of his friends.

HENRY BROOKS ADAMS

A Compassionate Heart

In this crazy me-first world, it's tough to find people
with hearts that are compassionate toward the needy
and downtrodden. You, my friend, are loaded with
God-given compassion. Your heart for others is
exemplified in all that you do. What a godly example!

Enjoying the View

A friend is one who sees through you and still enjoys
the view.

WILMA ASKINAS

A Consistent Walk

Lord, from sunup till sundown, I pray that You would help me walk a consistent path with You. May I not waver to the right or left or be blown around by every wind. Thank You for consistent friends, who lead by example in this area.

Allies

There is only one thing worse than fighting with allies,
and that is fighting without them.

WINSTON CHURCHILL

Dream Chasers

Thank you, my friend, for joining with me in my likes,
my dislikes, my passions, and my pursuits.
You've proven yourself to me over and over again.
I appreciate your willingness to stick with me no
matter which dream I'm chasing!

NOTES